AF487672

The tree of liberty must be refreshed from time to time with the blood of patriots and tyrants.

Thomas Jefferson

HOW TO BEAT DRUG TESTING

IN

THE AGE OF BIG GOVERNMENT

RICHARD GOLDBERG, B.S., M.D.

Table of Contents

Table of Contents Continued

PREFACE

This book is for informational & educational purposes only.

Any use of the information contained in this book is solely at the discretion of, and exclusive risk of the user. Any outcomes resulting from use of the information contained in this book is the sole responsibility of the individual using said information. The author, his affiliates, publishers, and any entity associated with him will be held free from claim, either by civil, state, federal, or other action, which may be sought as consequence of use of this books' contents.

By intent and action of reading and using information contained herein, the individual relinquishes any claim to personal harm or consequence, and further, any claim to pursuit of legal action against author/owner/publisher of this work. Any personal use of the information contained in this book will serve as individual agreement to indemnify and hold harmless the author from and against any claims, liabilities, damages, judgments, awards, losses, costs, expenses, fines, penalties, or fees arising out of or relating to use of said information, concepts, charts, or data contained in this book.

Copyright 2020. All rights reserved. Except as permitted under the United States Copyright Act of 1976, no portion of this publication may be reproduced or distributed in any form or by any means, or stored in a database or retrieval system, without the express written permission of the author, contributors, and publisher.

FEDERAL DEPARTMENT OF TRANSPORTATION TESTING – DOT

All transportation jobs with federal oversite have mandated drug testing done at **pre-employment, random, reasonable suspicion/cause, post-accident, return to duty, and follow-up** indications:

All DOT agencies are subject to this mandate:

FMCA- Federal Motor Coach Association

FAA- Federal Aviation Administration

FRA- Federal Railroad Administration

FTA- Federal Transit Administration

PHMSA- Pipeline and Hazardous Materials Safety Administration

USCG- United States Coast Guard

NRC- Nuclear Regulatory Commission

All individuals who work for these organizations are subject to frequent drug screening, as are military, and private workers in innumerable capacities.

Who DOESN'T have to be subject to random drug screening? Members of government such as the President, congressmen, and senators. Neither do doctors except rarely for pre-employment, and no testing exists for CEO's and other high-level executives. The mantra reasoning for drug testing is to preserve the integrity of safety sensitive work positions – if all of those I just mentioned don't qualify as safety sensitive, I don't know what does. Just food for thought about the inequality of current drug testing guidelines.

At present, all DOT testing is done as NON-OBSERVED. In other words, the donor goes into a closed room and urinates into specimen cup, then exits the room to give sample to collector. Testing collection is only OBSERVED if returns are required due to having INVALID RESULT, and for RETURN TO DUTY and FOLLOW-UP testing.

THE MOST EFFECTIVE WAY TO PASS DOT DRUG TESTS (OR ANY DRUG TEST FOR THAT MATTER) WHEN ACTUALLY PROVIDING YOUR URINE SAMPLE THAT YOU THINK MAY BE COMPROMISED, IS TO DRINK WATER IN THE 1-2 HOURS BEFORE THE TEST. THE AMOUNT SHOULD BE BETWEEN 1.5 AND 4 LITERS. THIS DILUTES URINE BY UP TO A FACTOR OF 8X FOR THE SUBSEQUENT 3-5 HOUR PERIOD.

AT PRESENT ALL DOT DILUTE-NEGATIVE URINES ARE ACCEPTED AS PASSING, WITHOUT REQUIRED RETESTING OR CONSEQUENCE.

Federal regulations specify that employers have option of accepting as negative or requiring unobserved recollection (majority of employers just accept as negative) – if they do request recollection, this has provided several days of additional time to washout so that likelihood of clean sample is optimized.

If giving another sample in such a circumstance, do not give another dilute sample, just provide sample without any aggressive pre-hydration.

HOW TO BEAT DRUG TESTS

Drug and alcohol testing programs were initially developed in the military and then spread to generalized government programs and ultimately the private industry. The original intent was as a 'deterrent' program – in other words, catch enough people that observed imposed consequences result in FEAR that will then prevent most others from using drugs in the workplace.

My intent is NOT to promote drug and alcohol use. Rather, my philosophy is that testing has become grossly invasive and over-reaching. I DO NOT believe anyone, or any organization, has the right to determine what an individual can or cannot do on their own time. Again, to be clear, I do not ever advocate drug/alcohol use while working (that would just be stupid). However, as particularly exemplified by long-persisting substances like marijuana, use while on vacation where it is legal a week (or more) before returning to work can result in a positive test and severe consequences. Testing has also been refined and defined to such infinitesimal detection concentrations, that Time of Detection (ToD) is severely encroaching on an individuals' personal time and privacy.

The purpose of this manual then, is to educate, and most importantly to help level the playing field for workers and the individual who believes in **FREE CHOICE**.

What you will find in this manual is not common knowledge. In fact, much of it is secreted and meant typically to be made difficult for laypersons to access. I have practiced in medicine for 26 years, worked as a Medical Review Officer, and I have over 20 years of experience in drug testing and toxicology.

I intend to lay out a bare-bones explanation of the drug testing industry, methods, ToD (Time of Detection) for commonly tested for drugs, detail of the MRO interview (should you test +), ways to avoid testing positive and cheat drug tests, and suggestions about what to do if you DO test positive. Simplified tables and graphs will be used for quick and easy revisiting as needs dictate.

THE FOLLOWING CHART IS THE MOST IMPORTANT IN THIS BOOK:

***Time that most common drugs can be detected in URINE**

Time of Detection (ToD)

Oxycodone	42hours
Hydrocodone	40hours
Amphetamine	72hours
Methamphetamine	72hours
Psilocybin/Psilocin	4-5days
LSD	Low dose2days, mod-high dose 4days
Cocaine	80hours
NMDA/NDMA	72hours
Heroin/morphine/codeine	72hours
Benzodiazepine	Variable (see below)
PCP	8days
Alcohol	1-2hours per drink
EtG/EtS	1-2 drinks 24hours, 3-6:48hours, 7-14:98, >14:120
PtE (blood)	3-40days depending on dose
Methadone	4-5days
Marijuana	Variable 1week-3months

***RECOMMENDATION:** Always try to give yourself greater window of time than chart indicates for greater safety margin.

Benzodiazepine: Diazepam 30days, Lorazepam 3days, Ambien/Triazolam 24hours. Varies depending on metabolite half-life.

RECOMMENDATION: Marijuana – avoid this drug if you have a Federal license or are subject to Federal testing. Just pick something else as it can linger too long with contemporary high dose strains, it's poorly responsive to dilution, and the testing sensitivity is too high.

***Times shown on graph are for typical or standard use. Extremely high dosage can extend ToD. All substances can accumulate in the body after chronic prolonged use, resulting in much longer ToD after cessation than shown on the chart – chart ToD represents single or episodic dosing.

****ToD relates to level cutoffs (confirmation cutoff) as standard for DOT tests for the following drugs **(because currently these are the only drugs tested for on the DOT panel):**

Standard DOT drug test panel

Drug	Confirmation cutoff
Amphetamine	500ng/mL
MDA/MDMA	500ng/mL
Cocaine	150ng/mL
Marijuana	50ng/mL
Opiates (morphine/codeine)	2000ng/mL
6MAM (heroin)	10ng/mL
Hydrocodone	300ng/mL
Oxycodone	100ng/mL
PCP	25ng/mL

A quick note about the current state of drug testing. Forget about analyzing half-life ($T^{1/2}$). Half-lives become somewhat meaningless in contemporary testing due to the SENSITIVITY of current testing methodology. A perfect example is Etg (Ethyl glucuronide-a metabolite formed in the body from drinking alcohol). Its half-life is 2.6 hours. By classic calculation, multiplied by 5 half-lives (I always do 6 for extra comfort margin) this substance should be long gone and impossible to detect after 16 hours. Yet, it is detectable for 5 DAYS in extreme cases! How can this be?! Well, think about the theory of half-life: halving a quantity over given time, in that theory then, the halving process could be infinite….. We know this isn't true exactly, but to a degree it is. When we look at elimination kinetics plots, drop-off of concentration occurs rapidly at first, but then one sees minimal changes in concentration over extended time periods.

EtG ToD in main chart assumes 500ng/mL confirmation cutoff. This is almost universally used to avoid high % false positives. However, 200ng/mL and 100ng/mL (various) assays exist. If these are used dosages should be halved to correlate to same detection times.

The sensitivity of testing now is to the point of a just a handful of molecules. In the case of Etg the immunoassays alone are detecting .000000001-.00000005 grams/mL of substance. If that's put into LC-MS/MS infinitesimally smaller amounts than THAT can be detected!! It's frankly ridiculous. Time of detection (ToD) then becomes dependent upon Level of Detection (LoD) of current technology. This is unlikely to ever change much from now because the sensitivity is already so extreme. Hence, I will refer to ToD (Time of Detection) throughout this text instead of half-life, as this is what matters to those concerned with avoiding positive drug tests.

Dr. Goldberg's lesson section on extended or high-quantity drug use

***yes, even alcohol**

People are often puzzled when they get a report that they have tested positive after what seems like a very long time has passed since their last use of substance x, y, or z. This section I have reserved to VERY CLEARLY AND STRONGLY spell out that if use has been such that complete clearance between uses has not occurred, drug can accumulate – this will effectively EXTEND ToD (Time of Detection).

The most extreme case can be seen with marijuana. A single use will likely only be detectible for 1 (or at most 2) weeks. This used to be 3-5 days with 'your dad's' weed, but marijuana is so potent now that I am seeing single use detectable for MUCH longer. If someone is smoking marijuana 2-3X/week for a few months, after their last use it will likely be detectable for 4-6 weeks due to accumulation (possibly longer). If they used daily for a month or more, they could test positive for 2-3 months! This is extreme with marijuana because it is a fat-soluble drug. However, even with water soluble drugs like amphetamine/methamphetamine, high dose or extended use can cause accumulation and greatly extend the ToD.

This brings me to my next point, which is high-quantity use. Common sense alone should be sufficient (not always the case....) to result in the conclusion: the greater the dose, the longer it will take to clear. The simple physical properties of greater = longer are one thing. This can be compounded further by exhausting metabolism or clearance pathways. As an analogy, if all the workers are busy packaging product, any surplus of product will sit and wait until workers are freed up to attend to that remaining product. This can create a 'reserve' of drug that is not being metabolized and consequently prolong the ToD.

In extreme use cases, THC has been detected in urine up to 3 months, and cocaine in urine for up to 22 days!

RECOMMENDATION: If use of ANY drug is heavy OR prolonged (without complete clearance between uses) allow significant additional time before submitting to a drug test.*

*For water soluble drugs 2-3 days.

*For fat soluble drugs 2-3 weeks.

RECOMMENDATION: Regular exercise maintains higher level metabolism and helps with quicker clearance of drugs. Aerobic exercise at 75% or greater heart rate for 30 minute or longer sessions will truncate ToD.

TARGET HEART RATE CHART FOR AEROBIC EXERCISE

AGE	75%	85%	100%
20	150	170	200
25	146	166	195
30	143	162	190
35	139	157	185
40	135	153	180
45	131	149	175
50	128	145	170
55	124	140	165
60	120	136	160
65	116	132	155

Any older, you should be retired and not subject to drug testing.

Dr. Goldberg's lesson section on hair testing

1. It is called hair testing, not hair follicle testing. The follicle is not involved in this process in any way, shape, or form.

2. Hair from the SCALP proper (when you get to the back of the head where the neck starts, this is no longer scalp) will show any drug used for a window back in time 3-4 months (-1week). The (-1week) means anything done in the week immediately before hair test submitted won't show because it hasn't grown out yet.

3. The reason the time period is 3-4 months is because the rules for hair collection specify that the hair collected is cut right up to the scalp, is measured out 3-4cm from scalp end, and anything longer is cut and discarded. Hair of the scalp grows at approximate rate of 1 cm/month, hence 3-4 months.

4. Any BODY hair (anything other than scalp) will show all drug use for past 1-2 YEARS!

5. Scalp hair can show much longer timeframe if from person with dreadlocks or extremely curly hair.

6. The darker the hair, the more it takes up drugs- thus smaller amount of use required to result in positive test finding.

7. New tests available that can detect SINGLE use LSD in hair. However, this is not commonly tested for, and would have to be specifically ordered.

8. Any drug can be tested for in hair but must be specifically requested. So very uncommon that LSD, mescaline, psilocybin/psilocin would be tested for without special specific suspicion cases.

9. Common hair test panels will be same as standard DOT panel: 6MAM, AMP/MAMP, cocaine, codeine/morphine, oxycodone, hydrocodone, MDMA/MDA, marijuana, and PCP.

RECOMMENDATION: DO NOT EVER consent to or allow body hair to be taken for testing.

If you <u>only</u> have body hair, shave one lower leg and allow to grow back in. Do not use illicit drugs one week before shaving or thereafter, and then only allow hair samples to be taken from that area specifically.

Hair treated by dyeing, bleaching, or permanent wave CAN have reductions of between 1-90% of drug concentration – this has been proven by controlled experimentation.

UV light exposure itself breaks down drug in hair, marijuana is particularly sensitive to this phenomenon. In one experiment, 11 (+) hair samples were kept in quartz container exposed only to daylight for 10 weeks. After this period, only 3 of the 11 still tested (+) when re-analyzed.

****See Pearls of Drug Testing for more information!!

Dr. Goldberg's lesson section on: Fingernail testing

Fingernail testing is essentially the same as hair testing in that the period of time that can be looked back is in the 3-4-month range. Fingernails are harder to influence any change on (as can be done with hair like bleaching to decrease drug concentration). Testing for any drug noted in this text can be done with nails, including EtG testing for alcohol use over last 3 months. For EtG to show up as positive it requires average of about 100-150 grams consumption of alcohol per week over the 3-month period prior to testing. This equates to about 1 drink per day 5 days per week, or the equivalent in binge sessions somewhat spread out over the 3-month time period.

One technique that may work, but has not been evaluated experimentally, is repeated soaking of hands/nails in dilute bleach solution. Multiple sessions would likely be required to effect a change, and soaking should be until penetration is evident by nail softness and flexibility.

Dr. Goldberg's lesson section on: What happens when you have a positive drug test?

You will be contacted by a MRO (Medical Review Officer) for interview. The purpose of this is to determine if there is a legitimate medical reason why you are positive, in which case the result will be changed to a negative/passing.

If you do not have legitimate medical reason, you may or may not be offered split testing. Even if not offered, it IS YOUR RIGHT TO REQUEST.*

RECOMMENDATION: If test is Federally regulated/DOT test, <u>ALWAYS</u> request the split test! Employers may or may not recover the cost for the split testing from you, and if **anything** happens to prevent the split from being completed, the test is canceled.

If the test is unregulated/private company non-DOT, it's dealer's choice. You are required to pay upfront for the split test cost. If it's a high stakes job or you just really want the job, consider paying for split testing.

*__Split test__ means bottle 'B' or portion of sample you already gave will go to different lab for confirmatory testing. Split testing is to LoD (Level of Detection), so they are not observing confirmation cutoffs – in other words, if the drug is there, they will detect it.

Again, the primary reason to request split is that if ANYTHING prevents this from being completed once requested, the entire test is canceled, and you will be asked to submit a new sample. This then should have given you plenty of time to get clean.

__RECOMMENDATION:__ Whenever submitting a drug test you think you might fail, DO NOT use any further illicit drug until report received back and testing complete. This way if test canceled, when you get contacted to retest, you will have had days to get clear and give a clean sample.

Dr. Goldberg's lesson section on: Standard MRO interview

Interview will start with introduction, and a request for you to provide identifying information.

Often a medical confidentiality disclosure will be voiced.

You will be advised of your drug test results, and then asked about prescriptions or any medical treatments that may prove as legitimate reason for you to be positive for substance x, y, or z.

IF you have prescription or medical records you will be asked to forward that information for review in one format or another.

IF you do not have supporting documentation you may be offered split testing (for details see **Dr. Goldberg's lesson section on: What happens when you have a positive drug test?** Listed above)

For INVALID/SUBSTITUTION/ADULTERATION:

The MRO will ask if you tampered with the sample in any way and will ask if you use illicit drugs. Obviously, never admit to anything.

If sample is INVALID, this means that SPECIFIC GRAVITY, CREATININE, OXIDANTS, OR PH were off enough to be concerning, but not enough to be sure that there was SUBSTITUTION or ADULTERATION, or there was IMMUNOASSAY INTERFERENCE (see **PEARLES OF DRUG TESTING** section). This may result in a retest, or request for you to give a new sample, or the test is canceled, and you don't have to retest. In other words, **INVALIDS are all GOOD**.

If sample is SUBSTITUTED/ADULTERATED, you will be offered option of SPLIT TESTING. The test will be reported out as a REFUSAL TO TEST. This is the same as a FAIL (or positive test without medical explanation) as perceived by the government or private companies.

Examples of what would lead to a SUBSTITUTED/ADULTERATED result would be adding bleach or soap to your urine sample or using a poor-quality synthetic urine that doesn't contain uric acid or has some kind of a preservative in it that the lab discovers, or diluting your sample with too much water.

Dr. Goldberg's lessen section on CHEAT URINES

If you're the type who prefers to just provide an alternative to your own urine, a sample known to be clean, there are 3 options:

1. Get urine from someone you can trust to be clean and keep frozen or refrigerated until use.
2. Synthetic urine purchased online (ie: Quick Fix, UPass, Clean Stream).
3. Freeze dried human urine (also called lyophilized).

Urine once at laboratory is tested for validity with measure of:

1. pH
2. Specific Gravity
3. Creatinine
4. Nitrite/Oxidant screen
5. Uric Acid- possible testing
6. BIT/E3G- possible screening, preservatives in some synthetics

If anything is done to urine that makes any of the tests too far outside of range of normal, the sample will be deemed INVALID, ADULTERATED, OR SUBSTITUTED.

REGARDING # 5: Newer test that only certain companies will request as this is only found in real urine and will reveal if urine is synthetic. Consequently, if they have this as component of validity testing and the synthetic used is not current or sophisticated enough to include it, it will be deemed SUBSTITUTED & A REFUSAL TO TEST/FAIL. *****AS OF THIS PUBLICATION {2020} THE DOT TESTING DOES NOT INCLUDE SCREENING FOR URIC ACID, SO GOOD QUALITY SYNTHETICS SHOULD PASS VALIDITY TESTING.**

BIT (benzisothiazolinone) & E3G (triethylene glycol) can be tested for and their discovery would indicate synthetic urine as these are preservatives not found in human urine normally.

RECOMMENDATION: I would advise only using freeze dried (lyophilized) human urine like Test Clear because it is real urine that you rehydrate so it is more likely to pass all validity testing. Synthetic urines can result in IMMUNOASSAY INTERFERENCE in DOT testing, which then requires you to go back for collection that is OBSERVED.

*Observed collections can still be done with cheat urines with prosthetic devices like the Monkey Dong synthetic urine device. However, if a collector for DOT has been properly trained, they will make you drop trouser, lift shirt, and spin in place to assure you are not wearing a device.

Most important factor when providing a urine sample is that it be at the right temperature, between 90-100 degrees Fahrenheit. There are adhesive warming packs that can be affixed to carrying containers to keep at correct temperature while you wait to give the sample. These warmers can easily be found on the internet. Heat initially with microwave.

Dr. Goldberg's lesson section on Saliva Tests/Oral Fluid Tests

Oral fluid ToD closely parallels blood/plasma.

Rough rule of thumb is that you need 2-3 days' time from last use of any substance to have negative test with oral swab.

Only thing that may help to pass oral fluid test is using sour candy, like Jolly Ranchers, to make yourself salivate profusely before and during the test. This has been shown to reduce drug concentrations by factor range of 2x-6x and could drop concentration below level of detection. But good luck, because if trained properly, personnel administering test will not allow you to have anything in your mouth 10 minutes prior to the test.

Also, if possible thorough tooth brushing and mouth rinsing before a test will be helpful in reducing drug concentration.

About the only good news is for marijuana users the detection time in saliva is only between 1-2 days, so not nearly as long as in urine. THC will be detectable for much longer in a chronic or regular user.

A final possible strategy is 'toothing' the sample swab. If the personnel administering the test give the swab to you and do not do the swabbing themselves this might help: only swabbing teeth or just holding swab in between teeth so that very little saliva is taken up. This can result in a negative/cancel as not enough specimen is captured for testing. Saliva samples are screened for albumin level (must exceed certain quantity for validity) or IgG antibody to assure sample is acceptable. New test kits are in development however that show saliva volume uptake and will not be considered complete until reading on unit shows 1 mL collection.

Because much of DOT testing may eventually be changing to oral swab testing, keep an eye out for the development of 'synthetic saliva' products to be used just like urine substitutes.

Dr. Goldberg's lesson section on Blood Testing

Blood testing is rarely done in standard drug screening. Usually this is done after motor vehicle accidents, or in chronic pain patients to confirm the use of prescribed chronic pain opioid prescriptions.

A special situation exists for anyone subject to alcohol abstinence monitoring. Blood can be sampled for **PEth (phosphatidylethanol –** specific RBC phospholipids formed only in the presence of ethanol). These are measurable/detectable after even single drinking episode for between 3 and 40 days depending on the total alcohol dose consumed. This value can also be correlated with hair concentrations of FAEE (fatty acid ethyl esters) and hair concentrations of EtG (ethyl glucuronide) to gage overall level of drinking: teetotaler, moderate social, alcoholic, or extreme.

PEth: light or no consumption <20ng/mL, significant consumption 20-199ng/mL, heavy consumption >200ng/mL

General rule of thumb should be that drinking once to level of buzz/intoxication would be detectable for about 3 weeks.

There are only very limited number of ways to manipulate or possibly shorten time of detection of PEth. Essentially this will amount to decreasing or diluting detectable PEth and increasing amount of new, unaffected red blood cells. The former may be achievable by donating blood, and then hyper-diluting one's blood by drinking mass amounts of Gatorade (or other solute-rich solutions) before giving blood sample. The latter stratagem requires some time devoted to exertion both aerobic and anaerobic, best if done at highest elevation possible. This will produce oxygen-deprivation stress that will promote release of erythropoietin (EPO hormone) by the kidney's, thus promoting new red blood cell production in the body.

Blood/plasma testing can be used to test for any/all drugs of note that can be tested for with urine screening.

Dr. Goldberg's lesson section on Breath Tests/BAT/EBT

Evidential Breath Testing Device

EBT devices used for DOT testing can distinguish alcohol from acetone at the 0.02 level – so Atkins or other diets, or Diabetic Ketoacidosis cannot be used as excuse for positive test (HAS been tried, and failed).

If you have a (+) EBT test (0.02 or greater), you are required to be tested between 15-30 minutes later for confirmation, after an airblank test is done.

It is your right to request all records showing current and accurate intervals for device external and internal calibration checks.

Frequency of calibration checks, inspection, and maintenance of devices is specific to the manufacturers plan and must be adhered to for the device to be qualified to produce actionable results. If guidelines have not been followed, test results may not stand up to legal examination.

Any inspection, maintenance, or calibration done on the device must have been performed by the manufacturer or a maintenance representative certified by the manufacturer, or an appropriate state agency, or the device is void.

Dr. Goldberg's lesson section on How Drugs Are Detected

LIQUID CHROMATOGRAPHY

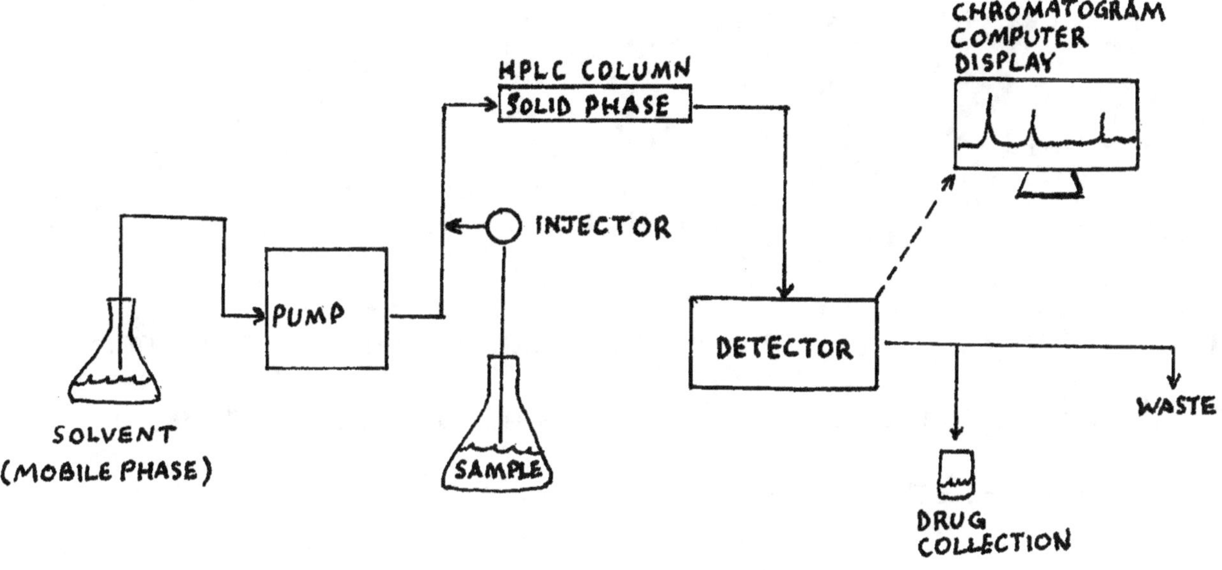

Mobile phase solvent flows at certain rate through High Pressure Liquid Chromatography (HPLC) column. Injector introduces sample to be tested into system. Flow rate of various components (drugs) through HPLC Column Solid Phase depends on size, polarity, and electrical charge of molecule, so separation (& hence purification) occurs.

HPLC COLUMN

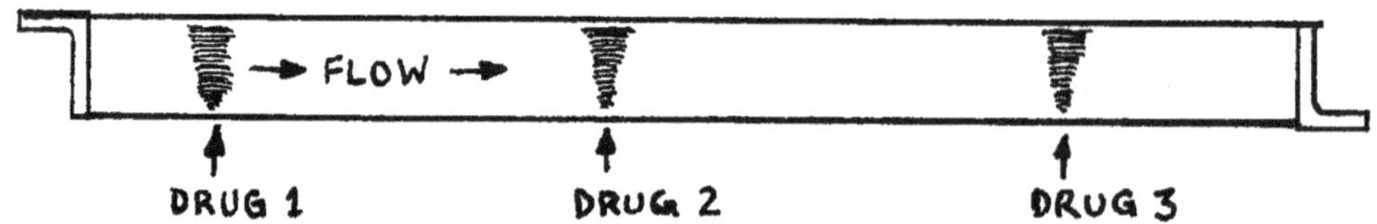

Detectors identify & quantitate the concentration of various components by multiple methodologies: UV light absorbance, florescence detection, evaporative-light-scattering detectors.

The detection by these methods is plugged into computer algorithm to display graphic representation. Identification is then possible by comparing to known retention times (tR) established by reference standards.

Further, the area under the curve can be used to calculate the exact concentration of the compound in picograms, nanograms, or whatever unit of measure desired.

After separation in the column, each compound can then be collected as a purified substance for further testing separately via mass spectrometry.

TANDEM MASS SPECTROMETRY

For sake of simplification, mass spectrometry (MS) and tandem mass-spec (MS/MS) can be said to electrically charge sample molecules, while shooting them through aligned magnets. This separates them based on charge and weight so that when they strike a detector they can then be 'read' against tandem reference standards. This technology literally directly identifies the exact, specific, unique molecule in question. This is done as confirmatory/definitive testing, and for practical purposes, essentially eliminates so called 'false positives' as cause of + drug test. This is the industry GOLD STANDARD.

PEARLS OF DRUG TESTING

Before any drug test, start drinking water about 1.5 to 2 hours prior. Drink 1.5-4 quarts. This will result in significant dilution of urine for up to 5 hours. This can dilute urine by a factor of 8X, which very often can decrease any drug to concentration that it falls below detection levels. Know that some employers or monitoring programs will require submission of another sample if 1st sample is too dilute. In many cases this is a strategy to allow you more time for clearance of drug so that the 2nd sample you submit is clean. Try not to give two dilute samples in a row as rare employers will exclude you from consideration for this (considered a FAIL).

Never admit to MRO (if interviewed) of tampering with a urine sample.* If you provided a synthetic urine substitute or use additive, these can sometimes result in immunoassay interference, which will result in request for you to submit a new sample (likely now to be directly observed by collection site witness). *If they knew, they wouldn't be asking!

Using synthetic urines (like Quick Fix) with some labs reagents will cause **immunoassay interference (IAI).** IAI means that something caused problems with first screening step of drug testing. This will prompt them to make you return for OBSERVED urine collection.

RECOMMENDATION: Use of powdered (freeze-dried or lyophilized) real human urine is better idea than synthetics as this is more likely to pass validity checks and result in a passing urine the first time.

Drugs/medicines that can block detection of various illicit drugs

The medications ciprofloxacin or levofloxacin can possibly block detection of oxycodone and hydrocodone.

Metronidazole (Flagyl) can possibly block detection of hydrocodone.

Ibuprofen at high doses can possibly block detection of marijuana.

Fluconazole (Diflucan) can possibly block detection of cocaine.

Aspirin can possibly block detection of various drugs or cause IAI. A dose of between 50-120mg/kg 1-2 hours before giving a sample.

Taking a dose or two (never exceed specified maximum dose range of aspirin) of the above medications 1-2 hours before providing a urine sample drug test MAY help prevent detection. Alternatively, it may result in an INVALID test due to IMMUNOASSAY INTERFERENCE (IAI), which will require you to submit a new sample. This will then have effectively gained you additional 2-4 days for further clearance of drug so that you can now provide a clean sample.

If providing a substitution sample (ie: synthetic, borrowed, powdered) the biggest rookie mistake that can be made is giving a **cold sample.** All sample cups have temperature strips on them and are always checked to assure that the sample is between 90-100 degrees F in accordance with body temperature. You MUST have the sample warmed (adhesive warming packs available on the internet) to the right temperature range, or it will be rejected. If rejected, they will make you stay until you can give a new sample, and if you leave it is a REFUSAL and hence, a FAIL.

Urine additives (meant to be added to urine sample during unobserved collections) are essentially all oxidants that can interfere with detection of drugs or break down the drug in the urine. When urine is sent to the laboratory, they are all tested for, and if found will result in ADULTERATED sample, which is a FAIL. This is considered a REFUSAL TO TEST. Examples include (stealth, urine luck, klear, clear choice, purafyzit, bleach).
RECOMMENDATION: Do not use additives.

OPIOIDS METABOLIC PATHWAY

Some opioids metabolize in the body to other substances. The arrows indicate UNIDIRECTIONAL metabolic change.

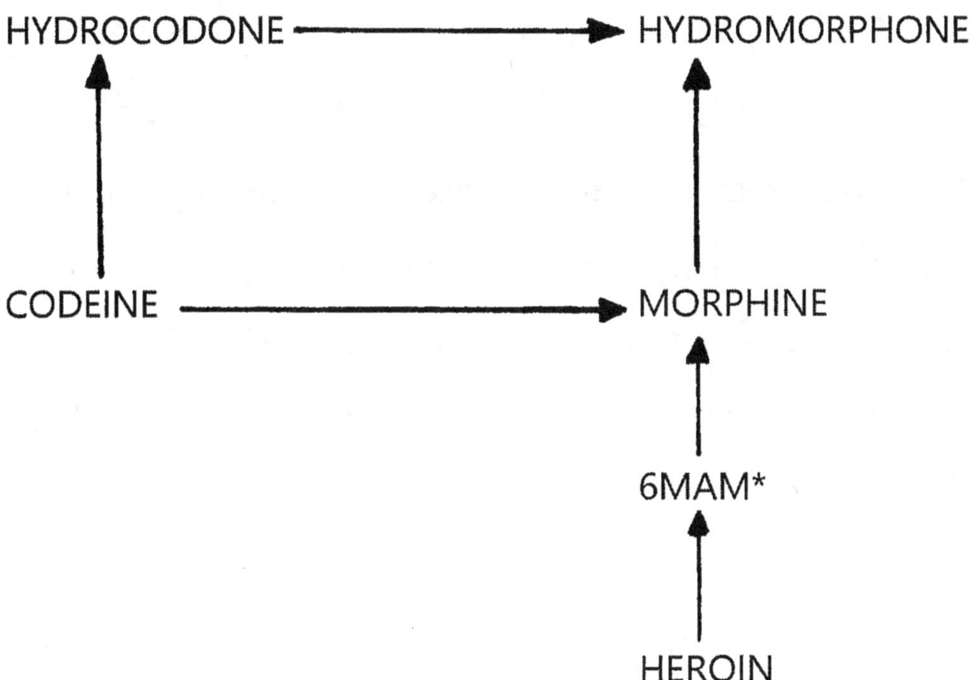

*6MONOACETYLMORPHINE- **only** comes from heroin

A good strategy for avoiding nasty surprises is to obtain your own drug testing equipment/kits to make sure you do not test positive before submitting to the real thing. You can also contact any of the major testing laboratories and test with them directly as a personal test (LabCorp, Psychemedics, Quest Diagnostics, Clinical Reference Laboratory). One of my favorite sites for purchasing testing materials is PharmaDrugTest.com, where you can find many different tests at reasonable rates. You can also find home drug test kits at any pharmacy or drug store for the commonly tested illicit drugs.

Keep in mind the **confirmation cutoff levels** may differ so you must keep a watch for these – meaning you could be testing yourself with a less sensitive test than the one they use at the lab. It will still give you a meaningful result and is certainly better than just guess-work. Just to reiterate, confirmation cutoff is the concentration at and above which the sample must be to trigger a test as positive. As an example: if you are testing yourself with a store kit that detects marijuana at 50ng/mL level, the laboratory may test at 40ng/mL level, such that despite testing negative with your home kit, you still test positive at the lab!

STRONG RECOMMENDATION: If you must give a urine sample for testing and are in doubt about passing, engage in aerobic exercise if you have time. One half hour or longer sessions, even one, can make a big difference. When you vigorously sweat, your skin is literally acting as an accessory kidney, filtering and eliminating toxins/waste products. If you think this doesn't make a substantial difference in elimination time, you are dead wrong.

STRONGEST RECOMMENDATION: NEVER GIVE A 1ST MORNING URINE. Make sure you have urinated at least once before giving a sample, and HYDRATE!

For that matter, you may even consider not giving first portion of urine. Begin urinating into toilet for a bit before moving collecting cup into stream. Fill to where they said to and don't give end portion of urine either.

Opiates (**morphine/codeine**): A word about these drugs specifically – if level is below 2000ng/mL for DOT testing it will not be resulted as positive at all. If > 2000 but < 15000 it will require explanation to MRO, **HOWEVER, IF YOU CLAIM EATING POPPY SEED MUFFINS OR CLAIM NO KNOWN SOURCE IT WILL TYPICALLY JUST BE OVERTURNED AND RESULT IN NEGATIVE TEST.** If the level is 15000 or higher you MUST have a prescription to provide for validation for the test to be reported as negative by the MRO. Private/non-DOT testing essentially adheres to the same rules and levels. **Bottom line here is to ask what the quantitation level was, then deny any source or claim eating poppy seed muffin/bread if it is below 15,000.**

Heroin specifics: This is the perfect place to comment on heroin, immediately following the above notes on morphine and codeine because of their metabolic relationship. Heroin use will result in a positive 6 MAM (6 Monoacetylmorphine) drug screen result (on DOT and most panels), but only if tested within the 8-10 hours immediately following heroin use. 6 MAM half-life is very short, about 30 minutes. If this comes up positive forget any other explanation, because heroin is THE ONLY SOURCE OF THIS SUBSTANCE ON OUR PLANET. All heroin is then converted to simple morphine and codeine in the body, and so those are all that will show up on a drug screen if done following the elimination of 6 MAM.

Hair treatments have been shown to reduce drug concentration in tested hair. One home method that can be employed is use of hydrogen peroxide. Just shampoo your hair normally, then following shampooing, wet completely with H2O2. Let it sit while you do the rest of your showering. Then just dab dry but let it stay in your hair and mostly dry naturally. Do this many times or daily before you know you will have hair testing done (the longer and more times this is done the better). It WILL lighten the color of your hair. This method will bleach and oxidize and can help to reduce drug concentration and detectability.

Another word about **EtG (ethylglucuronide)** testing for longer-term detection of alcohol use **in hair**. For quantification purposes, in America, a standard drink is 14 grams of alcohol (1 beer, 1 glass of wine, 1 oz shot). For hair test to read out as positive for EtG, the current level cutoff is 7pg/mg of hair. Studies have shown that at consumption rate of 100 g alcohol per week for prior 3 months (that's 85 standard drinks) the positivity rate will be about 20-25%. At 150 g alcohol consumed per week, the rate of positivity will be essentially 100%. **This tells us that one can safely consume around 60 drinks in a 3-month period to**

still have negative EtG testing in hair analysis. This has been confirmed with experimental testing at USDTL. The SoHT (Society of Hair Testing) has established the cutoff concentration of greater than or equal to 7pg/mg hair and this could be changed to a lower level, so make sure to do your own search to confirm that this is still the cutoff. At this cutoff one would have to have about 6 binge (to intoxication, ie: 12 drinks per) drinking events to trigger a positive hair result. A single drinking event (or even several) within a 3-month period WILL NOT result in a positive hair test.

Peth (phosphatidylethanol) blood level detection to USA specified +, considered >20ng/mL, will be attained by consumption of 2 standard drinks per day for men, or 1.5 standard drinks per day for women over past 30 days.

In general, the longest detection times for drugs are in hair/nails, followed by urine, sweat, oral fluid, then blood. Single dose of drug can be detected in blood for 1-2 days and oral fluid for 5-48 hours. Single use marijuana detectable in saliva only up to 16 hours. Chronic users of marijuana can be detectable in saliva up to 8 days after cessation of use.

Question of **single dose detection of drugs in hair testing**: very little
data exists. From what is available, the most likely drug types to be
detectable from single use include benzodiazepines and cocaine. Much
LESS likely to be detectable in hair from single use include: marijuana,
methamphetamine, MDMA, oxycodone, hydrocodone, and tramadol.
For the last 3 mentioned, it will usually take multiple repeat doses to
result in a positive finding.

Fentanyl is becoming much more prominent as cut in certain drugs
(cocaine & heroin), and illegitimately being passed off as various opioids
(like oxycodone) in stamped counterfeit pills particularly from Mexico.
As such, I mention here that a single use of fentanyl will be detectable as
the direct metabolite for 72 hours, and as the nor-metabolite for 96
hours. This is not on standard drug screens but can be specifically
ordered or inclusive in monitoring programs such as those for health
care professionals.

Don't waste your time or money on 'detox' or 'cleanse' products.
Virtually all of these include drinking large volumes of fluids in the
directions or mixed with the product. Water works just as well, and it
only matters in the 1-3 hour period immediately before the urine test is
given.

THE most effective way to hasten the elimination of drugs from the body is by engaging in vigorous aerobic exercise. The more times and the greater the duration this can be done before submitting to a drug screen the better.

REFERENCE LIST OF A PORTION OF SOURCE MATERIAL & SCIENTIFIC EXPERIMENTS PROVIDING FACTUAL BASIS FOR THIS TEXTS CONTENTS:

Axiomdiagnostics.com, Test True ™ Oxidant Assay

www.nbci.nlm.nih.gov 24819969, Detection time for THC in oral fluid

ISSN 1355-6215 02/040357-08, The pharmacology of psilocybin

Onlinelibrary.wiley.com/doi/full/1010.1111/1556-4029.13874, The PEth Blood Test in the Security Environment

www.samhsa.gov, Mean Detection Times

academic.oup.com/view-large/14364741, Excretion Profile of Hydrocodone, Hydromorphone and Norhydrocodone in Urine Following Single Dose Administration of Hydrocodone

academic.oup.com/jat/article/37/5/255/787330, Journal of Analytical Toxicology

doi.org/10.1093/jat/bkt031, Prescription Opioids I. Metabolism and Excretion Patterns of Oxycodone in Urine Following Controlled Single Dose Administration

www.ncbi.nlm.nih.gov/pubmed/27596747?dopt=Abstract, Phosphatidylethanol (Peth) detected in blood for 3 to 12 days after single consumption of alcohol – a drinking study with 16 volunteers

www.ncbi.nlm.nih.gov/pmc/articles/PMC4107122/, Ethylglucuronide and Ethyl Sulfate Assays in Clinical Trials, Interpretation and Limitations: Results of a Dose Ranging Alcohol Challenge Study and Two Clinical Trials

www.sciencedirect.com, State of the art in hair analysis for detection of drug and alcohol abuse

CNS Neuroscience & Therapeutics 14 (2008) 295-314, The Pharmacology of Lysergic Acid Diethylamide

http://dx.doi.org/10.1016/j.mayocp.2016.12.007, Mayo Clinic Proceedings, Clinical Interpretation of Urine Drug Tests

https://syntheticurinereview.com/quick-fix-plus/, Does Quick Fix Urine 6.2 Work? – An Honest Review Of This Brand

https://buyfakeurine.com/product/monkey-dong-synthetic-urine-device/?ref=1&campaign=udth2, Monkey Dong Synthetic Urine Device

Journal of Analytical Toxicology, Vol. 26, October 2002, Urinary Elimination of Cocaine Metabolites in Chronic Cocaine Users during Cessation

Journal of Analytical Toxicology, Vol. 24, October 2000, Elimination of Cocaine and Metabolites in Plasma, Saliva, and Urine Following Repeated Oral Administration to Human Volunteers

Journal of Analytical Toxicology, Vol. 37, Issue 2, 1 March 2013, Pg.s 83-89, Differentiating Medicinal from Illicit Use in Positive Methamphetamine Results in a Pain Population

Annals of Clinical and Laboratory Science, Vol.25, No. 4 1995, Mechanism of Interferences for Gas Chromatography/Mass Spectrometry Analysis of Urine for Drugs of Abuse

https://academic.oup.com/alcalc/article/42/4/317/160166, Sensitivity of commercial ethyl glucuronide (ETG) testing in screening for alcohol abstinence

Anal Bioanal Chem (2016) 408.2019-2025, Ethyl glucuronide concentrations in hair: a controlled alcohol-dosing study in healthy volunteers

https://USDTL.com, diverse resource for many aspects of drug testing

https://www.ncbi.nlm.nih.gov/pmc/articles/PMC3509610/, Phosphatidylethanol in Blood as a Marker of Chronic Alcohol Use: A Systematic Review and Meta-Analysis

2016 Consensus for the Use of Alcohol Markers in Hair for Assessment of both Abstinence and Chronic Excessive Alcohol Consumption

Clinical Chemistry 2009, Common Opioids Metabolic Pathway

www.ingramcontent.com/pod-product-compliance
Lightning Source LLC
Chambersburg PA
CBHW080919160726
48000CB00009B/3055